BLACK
GĪTĀ

Written by Dr. Rev. Solstice

Illustrations by Yanna Marie Orcel

With a Foreword by Jenna Anast

Layout and Cover Design by Niokoba

To Sisu & G

GĪTĀ CARTOGRAPHY

Divinely

Guided by Ngoc & Bantu

Foreword

I met Solstice not too long ago...if you
experience time as a linear thing.
I experience time in moments that have stopped
my breath dead in its tracks, in heartbeats in my
chest louder than drums, and in contagious laughter
with someone that wakes up the God in me, which
means by my calculation, I've known Solstice
for a while now.
When I first read Black Gītā, I was transported into
a journey inward. I noticed the blood coursing
through my veins and became aware of the tight
spots in my body that desired to release, and
through Solstice's words, I found a release that felt
like melting into a puddle of pure and sacred water.
Black Gītā is a sensual cosmic journey that
invites you to take a more in-depth look at the
relationships we cultivate with each other and
ourselves and opens you up to realize that those two
relationships are one and the same.
The words and images in Black Gītā remind you that
the one existing law of the universe is love, and the
sooner you surrender to that law, the sooner you
realize that you are pure gold.
Black Gītā gives us a chance to see the gifts the
universe has to offer are all around us, and my
invitation for you is to take note of all those presents
as you read, the ones that exist now and the ones
still to come.

Jenna Anast

THE COLOR OF

GĪTĀ
IS GOLD

Moon Call

fly me to the moon
where I can be happy and free
where there is no wind
to pull or push me

.Love.loves.love.
(Ah, if only Dwayne Michael Carter, Jr. Was a Neuroscientist)

Of course, my Love.
We've been led by generations of separation philosophy
that deemed humans inherently violent and evil.
Only now have these so-called thinkers started
 to understand the peace
  and love inherent in sentiment
   beings and the importance of joy and happiness.
    The separation ideology penetrated
     our books, music, television, schooling, families, relationships and all
      This world is beautiful, but lived through separation this world is ugly.
       This life is all we have and we have so much more than this life.
        The cloud over your head will soon turn to rain
         and that rain will nourish your roots and soil
          and you will grow.
           You will grow, my Love.
           You will flourish of contentment.
           You will rise with selflessness.
           You will expand.
            Expand far and wide, my Love, far and wide!
            You will shrink!
             Never in front of Another
             You will shrink under the stars.
            The moon will light you.
           No one will miss your presence because
          the moon will radiate its shine
         onto you and you will shine on all other Beings.
        And those other Beings will provide light for the heavens.
       My Love, that cloud over your head will provide light for the Heavens!

Oh my Love, the gift of pain is plenty and the art of mindfulness is infinite.
Skills, though, Love.
We need to develop skills in order to turn these clouds to light.
Forgiveness, a skill of only the gods is of utmost importance.
Become a God my Love, the Kingdom is within you.
To enter that Kingdom, you must forgive yourself.
And to take the throne, my Love, you must forgive all others
or you shall be the sole prisoner and the only guard of this kingdom.
Patience, though, my Love.
Patience will help you develop the skill of forgiveness.
Patience with oneself and with others, my Love.
Is there something more difficult than trust?
Trust for someone who now needs your forgiveness?
These skills, my Love, are interdependent.
Without one there is no other.
We should not claim to be a patient person if we cannot forgive.
Each can be developed through gratitude alone.
These skills are already your true nature
This is a course in remembering
My Love, remember to love.

Love loves love

Remind yourself: anywhere you are Love is
And Mirror That Truth in your every thought, word, action, encounter, and
Now
There is nothing to identify because everything is Love
There is no need for discernment, live by intuition.
When you are on the elevator, mindfully
tell those other riders you love them.
Smile.
At their perfection.

And they will hear your words at the edges of your mouth.
I speak to each of you with the understanding that
Ye is Us: There is no separation
I am because you are.

    You are because they are—we are many
     but we are one.
      In this Body of love
       You are the fingers
        that point to the moon
         the feet that moves us forward
         the eyes that feel the beauty....
        In this Ocean of Love
        We are the waves
       the ocean
      and the
     (Be)love(d)

    Love loves love.

Waiting Room Labeled "M"

It's already in front of me
And yet, I wait.
Wait for the magic that's happening
Wait for the moon that glows
Wait for the sun that shines
Wait for the love that's shown
I wait....for nothing.
It is here, yet I wait...

All Aboard the Autumn Express

listening to Nina
thinking
of our Night
Together
in a breathable sea
full of unimaginable
possibilities Guided
by our interweaving spirits
that form one unified
Spirit Of Power, Positivity, and Poetry
As we dance...
as we dance
Our dance
Never missing a beat
eyes meet eyes/
We find what we seek/
Eyes meet Eyes/
We find what we seek
Love loves love
For we find what we seek

For the Record

I love the journey

But the ending is my fav:

Hisses

Crackles
Crackles
Crackles

P
o
p
s

Romance Theory **vs** Erotic Intuition

Though she stood in silence, I melted there--serenaded by the melodic
vibrations of her presence/
My mind wandered downward to my vessel to confirm the essence/
She smiles, I blush, she kissed, I hugged. We talk, we laugh, we walk, we
love/

'Ah, Don't get too excited
Neither of you are farsighted!
Can't you see what you have ignited!?'

Yes, and, I am delighted.

Standing at the edge of the reservoir, her silence tells me she's more than
my paramour
She's paramount without a doubt, but this won't be won without a bout.

Standing at the end of the reservoir, her gaze tells me she's more than a
paramour, friends are fine and I can't be sure, silence I can hear but her
gaze says more/

This emotional gravity weighs on me like a flower on a rock and fits like a
key in the lock--ay, what elementary rhymes....
Let's get back to this dream of hers and mine/ let's look at the seams of this
clothed divine/as I stare at this box sitting on my shrine, I think.... "in time".
But time tells nothing, for time is timeless/poetry is poetry even if it's
rhymeless/love can't stand tall if the mind is spineless, alas, the time is....

'Yes, fine sir, love loves love, but why of it do you speak? Is not this
moment feeble and weak? She may be lost, but this is no time for
hide and seek.

You've kissed?!   You've peaked!

You're all Allure, mystery and I see pique! Haven't you the strength to stand
on your feet?

Love?
            What's next, a talking dove? *God's a Girl* and determined your love?

Love?
            You mean infatuation?
            Professional castration?

Love?
Where ...'

In her eyes.
When she rubs my head and I her thighs.
Cause my lips...my lips can't even form lies.
Cause even saying 'hi' I get tongue-tied, every sight of her is like a surprise.
She's the sunset to my moonrise
I'm darkness but her fire flies
I'm an endnote, she's my reprise/
baptized
in the sky of her eyes/

This is not infatuation
nor witchcraft
these words had no revisions or rough draft...
I just wanted to say that...
i/I...

Soft Friendships

Ride straight....
Wheels covered in mud, their handlebars thud as the path is absorbed....
'Ride straight' he reminds himself.
It's a-okay to drift...he slept.
The dreams were no better, as the bike tilted and the path withered, but
with the Moon, she weathered.

She rose.
Mind grew within her heart as she touched souls.
Heart grew within my mind as she engaged my eyes, ears, throat, and nose
The taste of friendship sung sweetly through prose
For you, a rose.

Goddesses

We sat there below the bridge
We ate the wind
We circled the rain
Blue skies, deep sea

The Need to Want One

I want you.

There is a difference between need and want.

I know.

Melanin Lights

"Red!"
    With His open hand extended forward
      He tried warning me...
        ....us:
          "Stop" *Are you ready for what's to come?*
           We waited in smiles, frozen steel side by side
            (Un)authorized
             by the youthful melanin that graced our presence
            with wisdom.
             Halting us in a moment of playful inspiration
             We stayed.
              pressing for the yellow light
              While other adult children pressed for green
              His eyes gazed downward as he walked away
              Pacing in thought: *Are they ready?*
              Returning, decidedly
              He gave us His blessing.
              We carried on, Together
              Moving in place, still, slowly
             Finding ourselves surrounded by moons
            Unalienated
           and
          Unphased by Scullian Ex-Files
         Hand planted gently in hand
          Protected by the Elephant's Memory
        We danced in toothless laughter
      Resting gently, the boy smiled, knowing the two are in good hands

    Next Stop: Chizelle's Place.

Red turns Yellow

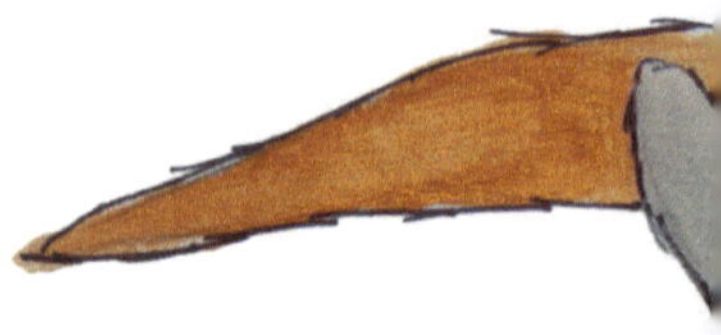

Seasonal Love:
An Interlude

falling in love
makes us spring into action
but too often we do not
bare the winter
though even some who do bare it
are frightened
when love's larva shifts and changes
so instead of
seeing the chrysalis
as a womb
they see it
as a grave

................not us.

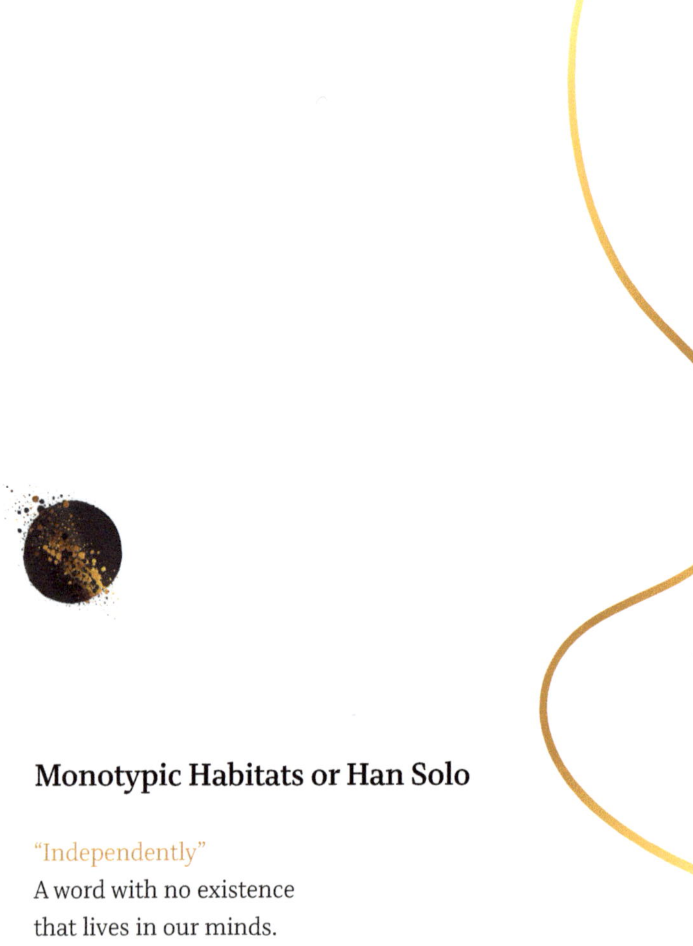

Monotypic Habitats or Han Solo

"Independently"
A word with no existence
that lives in our minds.

We Turn Together

She held my hand
and
for a moment
I felt like dirt
then like the relief of pulling a splinter out of a
finger;
a flower grew between our clasping hands
the stems
wrapped around our knuckles
tightening our grip
roots
expanded
around our bodies
pulling us
together
our bodies (e)merge into a spaceless, timeless place
stems continue to grow, several for each limb
we turn green
our lips morph into scented petals
our eyes into budding seeds

suddenly
 bees surround us, their stingers dripping honey
  the colony begins to do a waggle dance
   and dance round round us
    releasing honey
     sliding slowly down our rooted body
     anchored melanin
      we turn gold
       limbs mutating into bark
       birds appear
       resting on our shoulder
       singing
      the sun rises
    skies turn purple
this is only the beginning....

Her Body

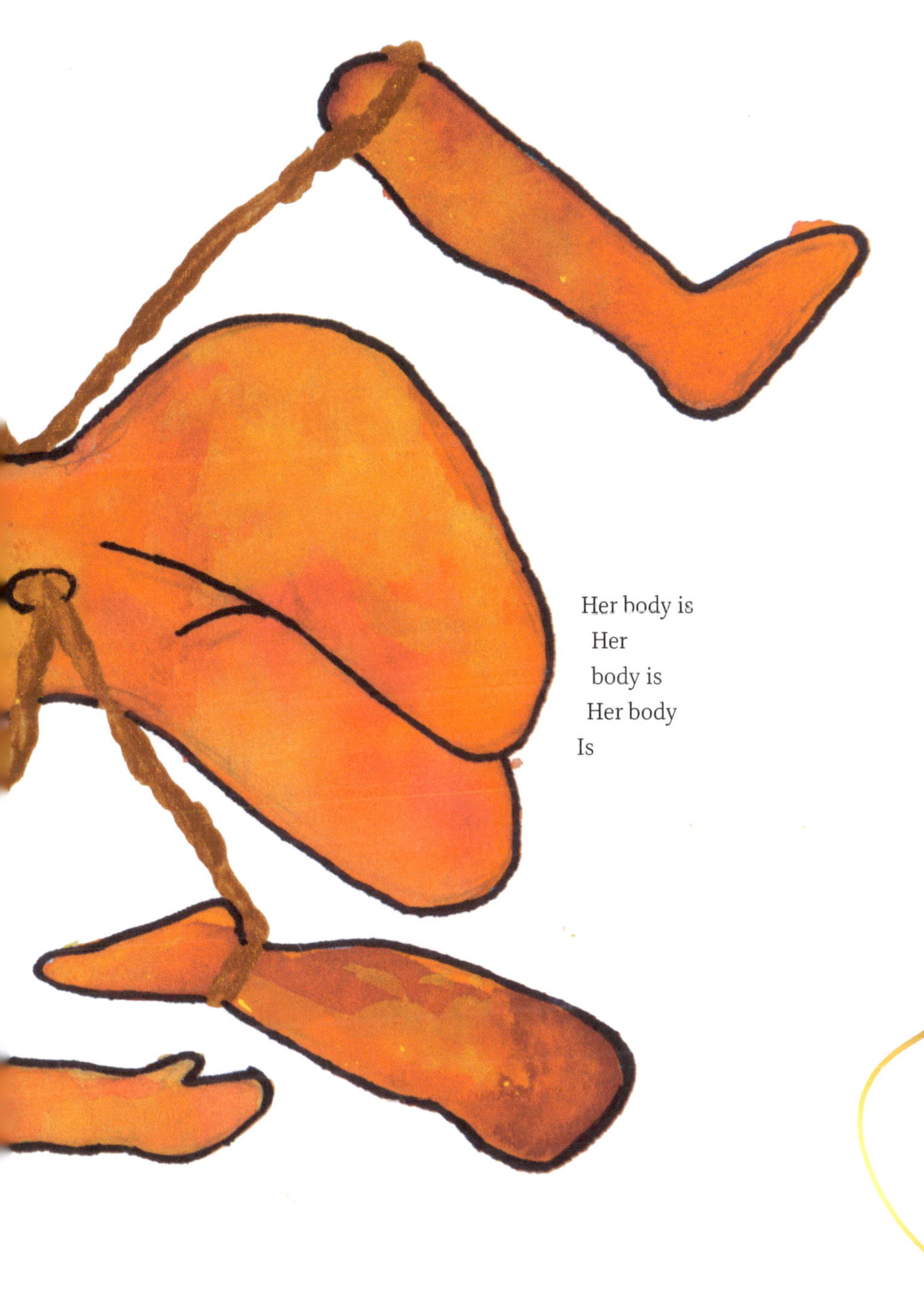

Her body is
  Her
    body is
  Her body
Is

Rain

The sound of the rain is comforting
As is the feeling: soft and hard
As the lightning slips in and the thunder bombards
The wooden surface drenched matching our bodies
As we match our bodies
wood and drench
fire in water
Nervous of a neighbor's glimpse
While I stand and you bent

a universe in arch

floating planets waving
cemented and far from asphalt
 matching the sound of the rain like a flower in the sun.

A Neighbor's Rainy Day

I seen them.
They knew I seen them.
Their masks slid off
They danced so beautifully, then.

Bravely, that is.

There was only energy
a gold star shredded its fairy dust along chunks of mask
atoms slowed down
and all that mattered was the crackling from the record
The song ended.
Joplin died.
And there are no Big Brothers around to
Hold my tears that are 50 years late.
And, now
it was time to end the dance.

Incomplete

We are in complete without our opposites

We are in complete with them

The Need to Want Two

I want *you.*

There is a difference between need and want.

If i needed you I would be your
prisoner
wanting you...

I am my own.

A Muse for You

Everyone is a Muse and a Creator

The Muse
muses   and muses   and muses

And the effect of Her musing is Her own Muse—

> *Her Enlightening Is*
> *Her Enlightenment*

Made from Her own pouring of Light into the cups of others
Her Words are the Gold to their Crown.

Then and only then can I truly command.

i/I

It was then
when i began
to cry
after seeing you hurt
that I realized
i/I am because you are

So Many Tears II

What am I trying to water
What am I growing
What seeds are there planted that's
Siphoning
My shell's tributary
Weaving my roots in the astral bloom

A Galaxy looked my way, pointed to my forehead and said:

There is the eternal gardener

And life is its infinite florist

Soil your mind with Love and Gratitude

And your field will spring into a botanical Paradise

Sun by Day, Phoenix by Night

Let your inner phoenix be your only constant
See no night
as your fires burn
the past
in the evening hours
before dawn
reborn
in perfect presence
winged-pyromaniacs
asleep in every waking soul
becoming a warm glow
as the sun rises in its place
letting you know that today's a new day

—ye is us.
(i am because you are)

Question and Answer
is a relationship between two lovers—
sometimes they quarrel
sometimes they
create—
sometimes their quarrels lead to the most passionate of creations.

There is no separation.

The Answer Commands:

Make love to me,
    for I am the Answer
    that you crave
    and thus
    I am The Lover, Your Lover
born to end Your existence.

The Question Speaks:

I exist because You exist
together We are the flapping of the wings and the chaos that it brings
You are the butterfly to my caterpillar
Love Me to death!

SPACE

EVERYTHING

Erotic Foresting

Lost and found in the forest of her love

I stand still

The trees of her soul give life
Her face
landmarked with wings
that guide me to the milky ways of her eyes.

    We stand still

        Together
         Healing

         Healed.

          I meditate in the stillness of her passion.
         We are finally here
        The Cosmos are passing
       Affliction is fasting
      Happiness is lasting

Lost and found in our beam of steaming light

We shine

El Elefantito

Remember when you were born?
Your lily-scented tears flowed endlessly
melting into our arms
and
quenching the fire we so desired
with the penetrating eyes of your mother that could pierce even the devil's
ears
with **rhyme**:

      a relationship between words that create a melodic symmetry
      building memories of oral motion

Your Mother's voice resonated as your cries scaled the octaves
inviting neighbors and mail-carriers alike to gather round our house
joining in your tearful speech
serenaded by Unconditioned Love

Ay, mi Elefantito...

the door opened
and you were treated like the most precious of Blunts
kissed and passed, kissed and passed
Your soothing touch birthed an orchestra of awes
your small motions gave rise to a movement of law
that said,
"Love is the law, Love is the only law"
finally,
the bees returned...
waggling.
honey-soaked stingers ready
circling us in the air
honey flowed, splashed, splattered, and drowned us in a new branch of life

We *turn* Together

Virgil's Meditation

In the beginning
I sat on the shore, wishing
I could be one with the water.
In love with its continuous calmness-

Breathe in
I am a Wave

Breathe out
I am the abyss-

Encircled with roots
My feet becomes tangled yet I felt free
My mind reflected the lake's blue depth
I no longer wished
i just was and then I was not
As a bird glided across the surface
the ripples birthed a smile.
Silence danced.
There was no beginning, no shore, no roots, no present, no end.
Everything was no thing.

Lake Triquetra

...and then i became nothing
there was no me, no her, no lake
just the Oneness muhammad and jesus agreed on at buddha's request
The waves, the smiling birds, the dancing roots, the silencing blue,
the encircling abyss, the breathing shore, the calming ripples—all
becoming nothing

Emptiness achieved

he smiles, He sees
she dives, She breathes
they cease.
Surfacing anew
she wipes Her face
"Ye Is Us," She says
He Sees, She Smiles
He Breathes, They're found
They dip love in the water
Writing open messages using earth's ripples
Circling our worlds
as Dante watches from ashore
Releasing us from *Eye's* circles
Burning down our egos
using the ashes as the batter that
bakes the 7-terrace wedding cake
in Celebration of the Holy Matrimony of
Inferno, Purgatory, and *Paradise*
Ah, praise the Circles of the Holy Trinity!

Believe.

To know the ledge is power.
Leap.

An Interlude: Are You a G.O.D.?

INT. SEA – DAWN – CONTINUOUS ACTION

Looking up at the Waves, calmly, down from the Seafloor, unfolding in unity...

Ngoc & Bantu: *Ye is Us.*

Ngoc: Through Love there is no separation, i am because you are. Thrice the answer repeated.

Bantu: What exists that is not love? What breathes without Goddesshood?

Ngoc: Nothing is without love and only nothing. Everything is God and God *is* everything.

Bantu: But what of "Devils," my Devi?

Ngoc: God is to Spirit as devil is to Ego
God *is* master of Joy—
Heaven.

Devil is servant of fear—
Hell.

Many of us are devils—
those of us loyal to the Ego
          housed in the body—spaced
          slave of pastfuture—timed
          led by the (un)Holy Quintet--sensed

All of Us are God—those of Us
          That Are.

Bantu: Are you a **God Or** Devil?
Love or Fear?
Present or unaware?
Trice the question repeated. Nonce the dichotomy defeated. We are One.

Ngoc: Those guided by fear must visit the Pynk Florist at Lake Triquetra.
Love will teach them the languages of the Solstice and their only law will
be Love; Love is the only Law. Even in the Blackest of Autumns. In all the
colors of the Song they will Unfold into Us and be ever and free.

Bantu: Where is this to be sung and what are we to call this Song of Black
Gods?

Ngoc: All is sacred. All is mundane. We are in Divine Order. Remember,
Bantu, my (Be)Love(d), we are Goddesses!

And this is *Black Gītā*.

Nature's Home

it was deep, yet so gentle,
Their sleep.
usually, their passion(s) kept their spirit's windows open.
never have I been such witness until that day....

the gold colony,
unseen since the Elephant's arrival,
waggled silently
into a waterfall formation.
As layers of honey reigned up,
flooding the land
Me and the Love that gave me life
assumed our tree pose

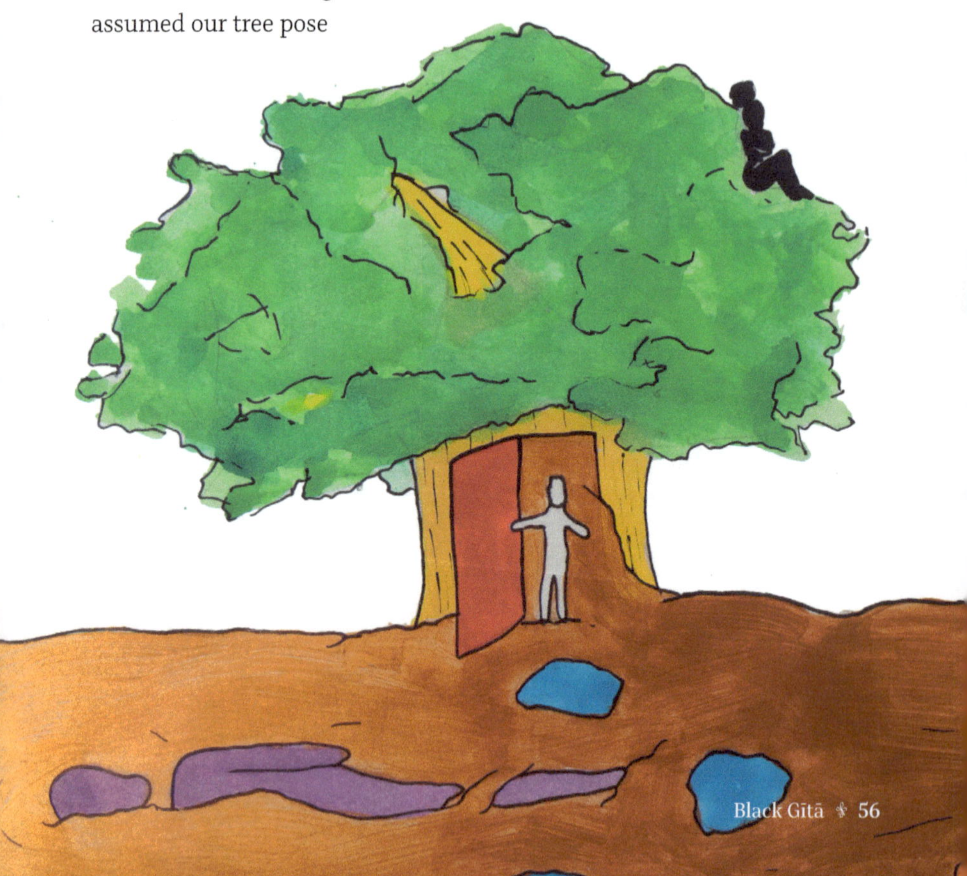

while our vision of a home
unfolded by Nature's literary golden prose

the sun rose
heated honey crystalized
lavender trilogies bourn untold
the porous hexagonal structure evolved
as its gaps stretched
far and wide
forming our home's lungs and eyes.

Taking swift melodic flight,
the purple colony
danced their way around
with their green, honey-infused stingers,
soiling the dirt
dabbing the periphery
where the trees and garden will grow
as various shades of honey
echo with capillarity
through the covered seeds.
roots emerge
creating *an intertwining of sorts*
then dangle
from the spawned tree
for the singing elephant to swing

16

...of us sat in a circle of strangeness, unity, and connection.
In just
a few short days
we moved each other
Her wrinkles; they parlayed across Her face
gently and randomly with precision

I waited for Her to speak in the Circle

some days she didn't

Her words tapped danced, creating vibrations in the room
With each word, gesture, change in expression
her wrinkles formed to wings
melodically
flowing across the map of her face
outlining the cartography of her emotion
Her eyes forming bridges
The ley lines live in her forehead as the wings guided the rest

But it was when she smiled

when she smiled...

that the lines all connected
shadowing
the edges of her lips
engaged all
wings and made my soul take flight.

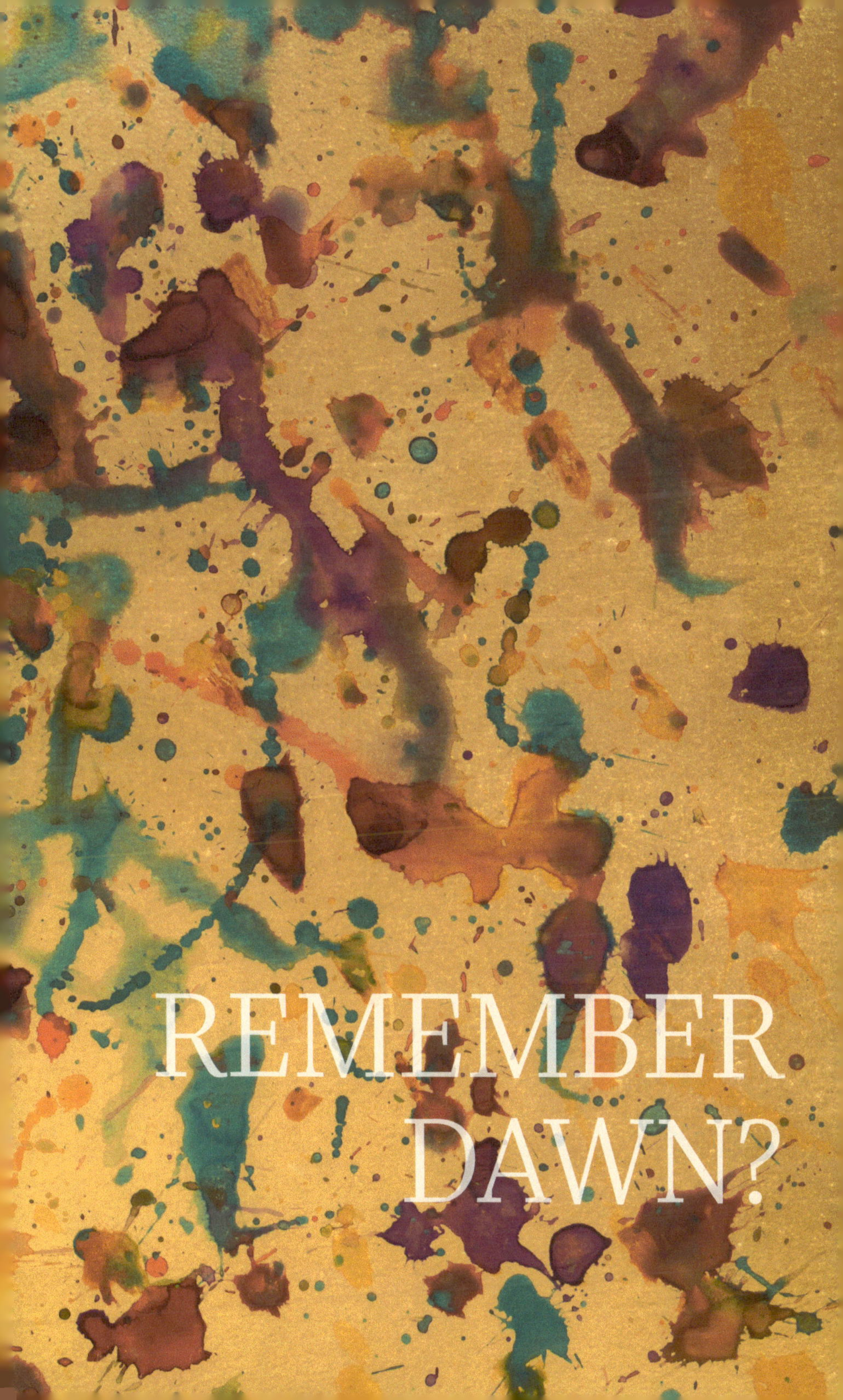

REMEMBER
DAWN?

SEE HER

Memory Kindness

Memories never die
but
we do
need some
kind of refurbishment
to keep them
from losing
meaning

Pleasant Overtakings

Her scent carries my day
away
through euphoric, redolent aroma
as the taste of her Labyrinth gentrifies my migrating tongue
The fire of her eyes
soaking
my palms
Pulsing
matching the rhythm of her yonic heartbeat
cultivating my Bodhi Tree for the soiling of Her own Eden

The rain continued...

my iridescent bark
Roared
to the convergent throbbing
of Our overtakings

the rain took hiatus

but the flooding continued
....pleasantly

as we nested our Love
in *Nature's Home*

Overtook.

Resting on the nightstand, they pierced my eyes. I smiled.
A part of her remains.

Laying there, tangled
Hooks touching like a pirate's agreement...
She's here. I smile:

Ye is Us

A part of her remains.

Dancing aside her cheeks
Long, Dangling
Sweeping across my hand
A part of her remains

Yes, her cheeks
Those dimples that make me weak
Soft. Smooth. Ah, the heat.

Uno
dos
tres

Leap

¿Que clase de mierda es esta?

YE
I

US
S

Nature's Home II: El Luna Colony

Nightfall hinted at a candlelit honey dew
but more bees arrived...
Glowing
like white fireflies

"el Luna colony..."

We became silhouettes
to our own bodies
as their thick iron honey fell
forming small titanium-like pebbles around our feet
Flowing smoothly across
the honey-dried floors
Crashing against unopened boxes
some clustered into Winnie-size bowls
some remained small.

Our shadows disappeared

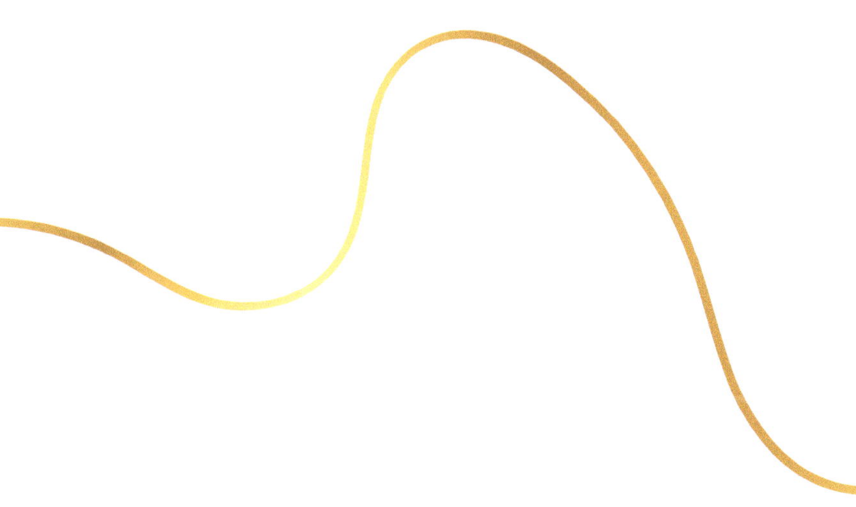

the bees reverted
to a pale yellow
forming a circle
round the three of us

a lunar basalt grew as our pupils approached miosis
rising to the height of our halos
it propagated and crashed into all four honey walls
pervading the blueprints
the Moon Bees gave us light

Now,

We turn ...

"Elefantito...?"

"Sorry Ma, did I wake you?"

"No, babe; but don't tell them just yet. Our Turn is Tidal..".

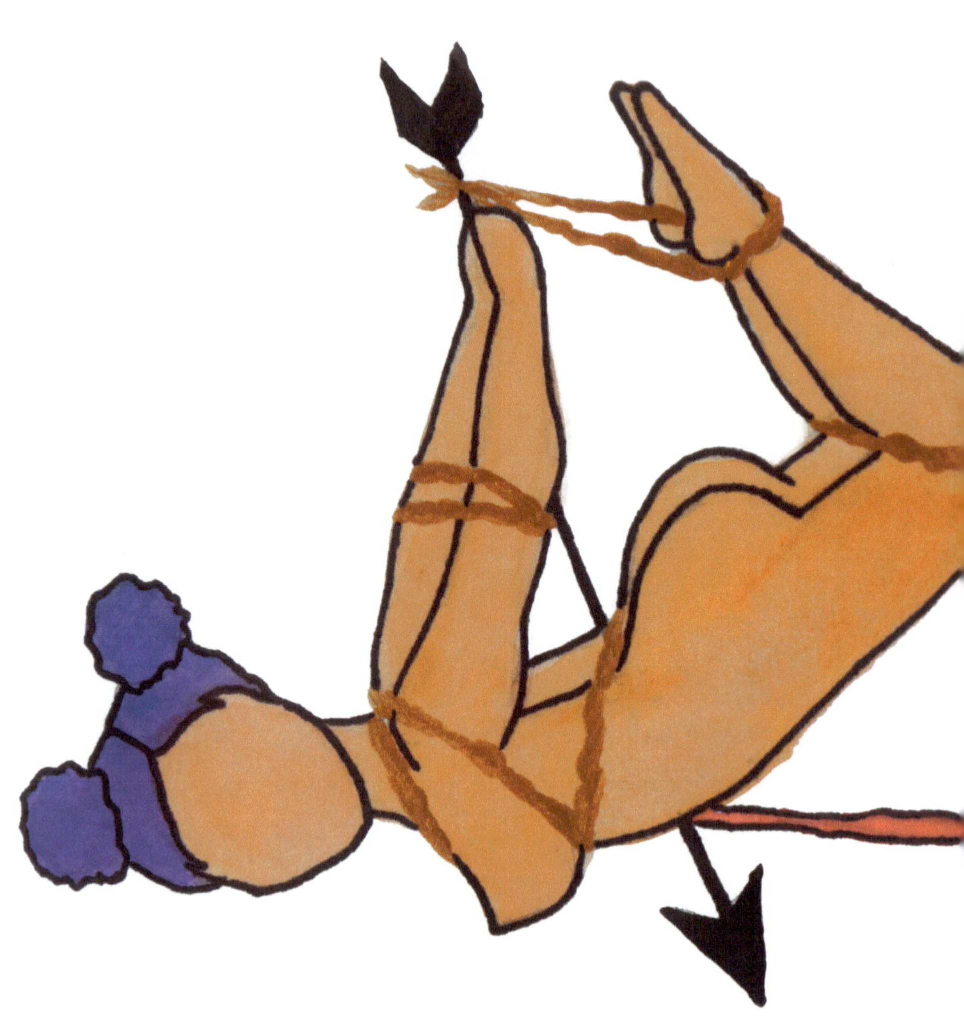

Arrow

Even the arrow requires multiple directions

it cannot fly forward
unless
it is first pulled back
pain, learning, and healing
oscillates
and it is not linear

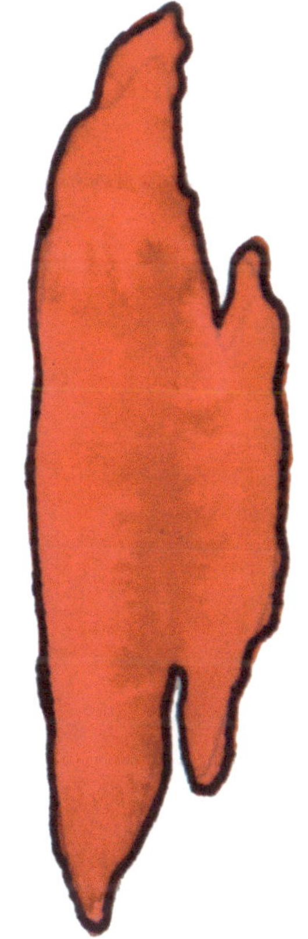

Dancing Buddha

let your emotions be musical
let them
dance
to the rhythm
of your
silent mind

The Need to Want Three

There is a difference between need and want.

If i needed you I would
be your prisoner
wanting you...

I am my own.

Being with you without
requisite or wanting...

We are Free

WE
ARE
MANIFESTIVE
BY
NATURE

Torquiest Galaxies

i sometimes space out when I look at you
in those moments
gravity
becomes my enemy
as
i just want to float
into the galaxies of your eyes

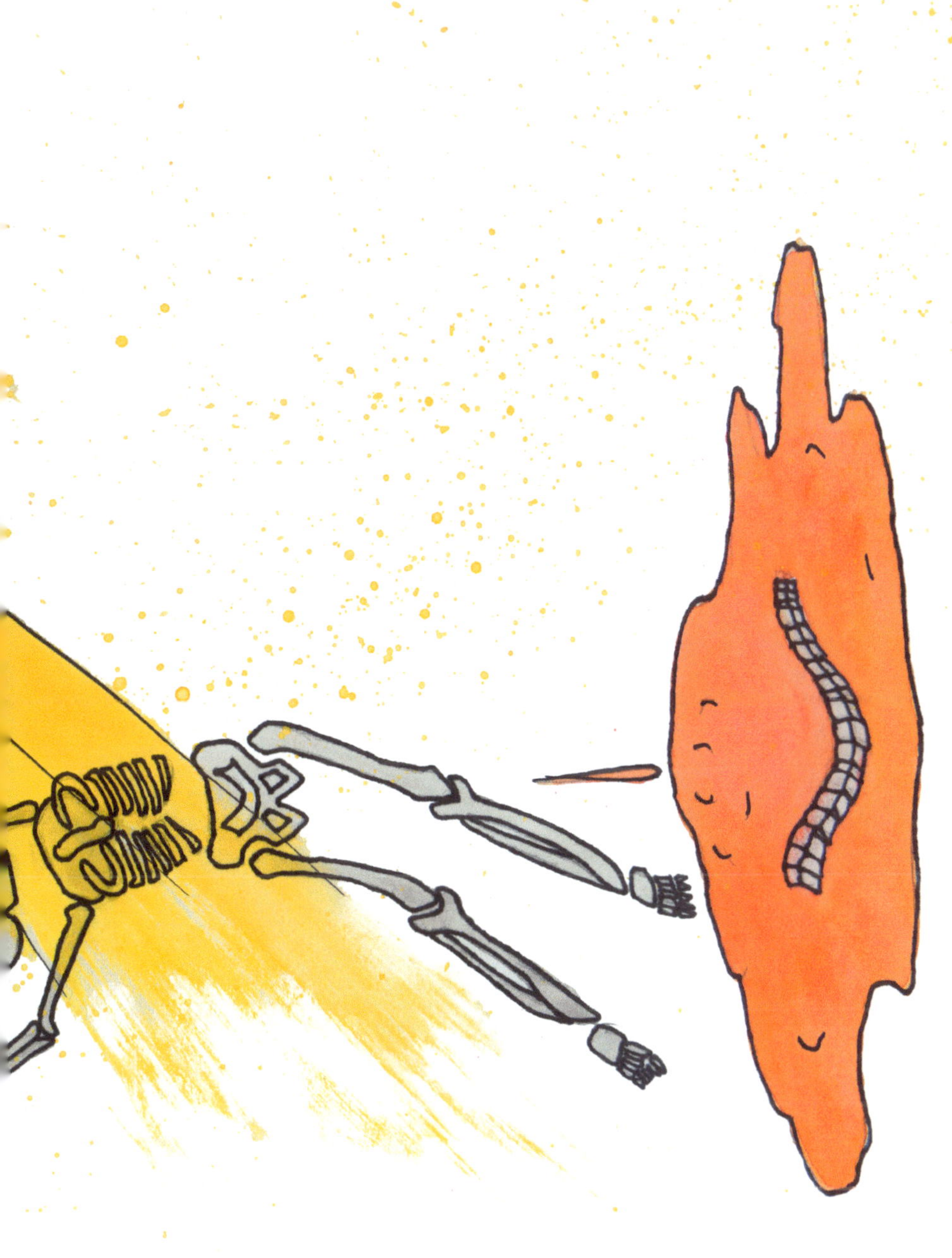

Dusty Telescopes

 She saved me.

Released
in a fleeting instant
from my most crippling of lies

And, so it crumbled

The smudge of darkness no longer
(O)n the telescope of my inner being

Moon Children Unite!

Coupla Fears

my fear of fear has brought me fear-
less makes me smile from ear to ear

Seaport Shells

I can hear it
That Oshunic guidance

I hear it in the Seas when they dot the Oceans
I hear it in the reefs
when the seagrasses make our blue carbon pollen prairie beds from deep

Love comes to fruition
Fruition only comes from Love

Bountiful in seed
blooming of a gilded promise

I found seaport poetry
Ashore to a golden sea
unlost, unclaimed, moving steadily
across the harbor while everyone watched
the night pass with Orion's
three sisters shining
like the Sea's moonlit dots and ripples

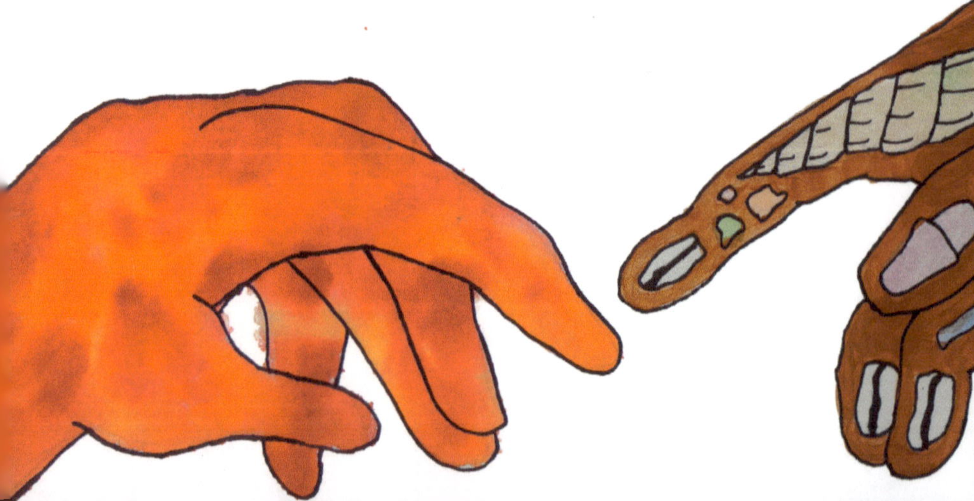

mirroring Her smile of dimples
her rising cheeks
opening to a waterfall of seashells
that I attempt to reach
just before our tips meet
my body turns to lava from hands to feet

...my ashes are plenty

Moon Calls are many

Howl.

A Golden Lava Sea
Almighty and Free

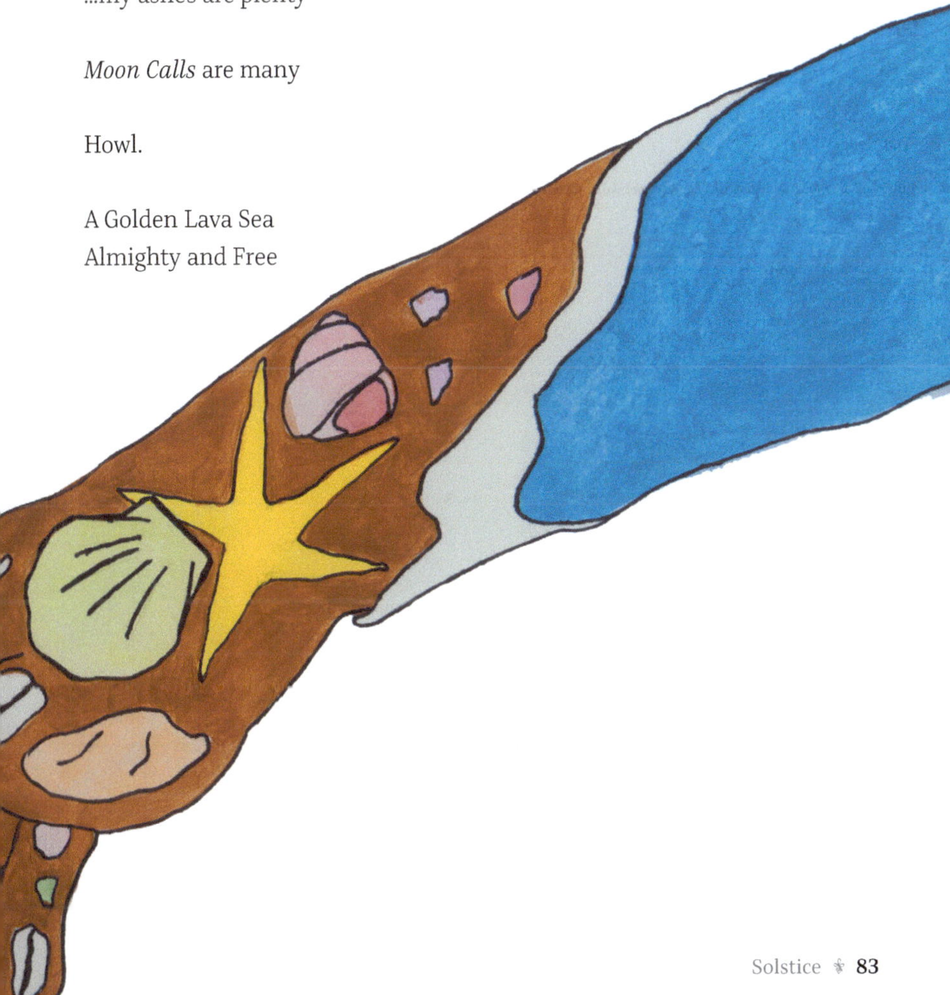

Ordinary Beauty

the decoction from our vessel
rushes through
my mound
so I can take flight
reaching
for you
wrapped in purple velvet barkcloth
pulling the anchor
down.
with vulnerability
and empathy,
cementing it in wax
with passion and power,
sealing it
with rhyme

Ye's Mirror

Love loves love
and Love is like a friend to me
and friends are like reflections
so it's important that
I love me

Oceanic Lifetimes

I blinked and seen Love tucked underneath my eyelids
    painting the darkness with a lasting togetherness that transformed
    a blink into eternity
    darkness into light
tears into deep waves

    of joy

that washed over my soul and united it with its timeless other.

As our two souls merge into one ocean
we ripple across in smiles
I am Hers
   and She is Mine
   and We are One in all lifetimes.

Ma Wa Tongued
(Languages of Aphro-Thelema)

I was once a student of life
asking and searching for the answer(s).
But then I met a learner seeking transformation
understanding
that even when knowing the answer, if the mind isn't transformed,
it remains in vain.
students are logical,
learners speak through love.
Inseparable. Though:
(Students must learn and learners must be students).

In logic there is right and wrong—
dualities. (You see, I am once a student of life)

In Love,
there is nonlinear growth and rebirth

Speak through Love
not mere logic

Realize
Love
is the only logic—
the only law;
Love is the only law.

Love Is

Love at the end of the day
Can seem tired

can still have energy from the day, keeping you up

Love
at the end of the day
Is the only law, Love is the only law

Love
at the end of the day is what makes the next day
excited to come
and the present day sad to go.

Love
at the end of the day
can shake your ego and provide it with the
painfullest of headaches

....and heartaches

Love
at the end of the day undermines and helps destroy
your ego

Love is like that: an ego-destroyer.
 One of the nice ones.
  One that at the end of the day knows
   exactly what you need and how you need it
   An ego-destroying light that gets you
   through the end of the darkest of days
   Revealing the beauty of the dark
   Itself in the dark
   Itself as the dark
   Its Self

  Love at the end of the day is Love and Love
 is the only law.
 Love is the only law.

Love is

0:00am

Stars wouldn't be as beautiful
if they weren't in the sky
As piano keys couldn't grace your ears
without a string's tie

I've experience heaven on earth
with you in my life

So
me without you
the sky will fall and the strings are cut

A seedless soil
watered with the sadness of a lifetime love that didn't live
to fully blossom

Remember

She lay my head on her chest
and said:

Remember,

*We Are
Goddesses!*

Meeseeks Simone

I intend to be independently blue.

for you.

Quantum Union

I was captured.

Her sound held me in place while Her body completed The Spell
Her Shelter made it feel so that my energies could dance past the edge…
Knowing they were Loved
and thus edgeless.

…She knew I was edgeless.

She released the wings I caged as feathers

And whispered:
    Ye is Us

I flew Godward.
In complete obedience to the only Law that exists

My Flame one with Her Voice

The rise demanded rubble.

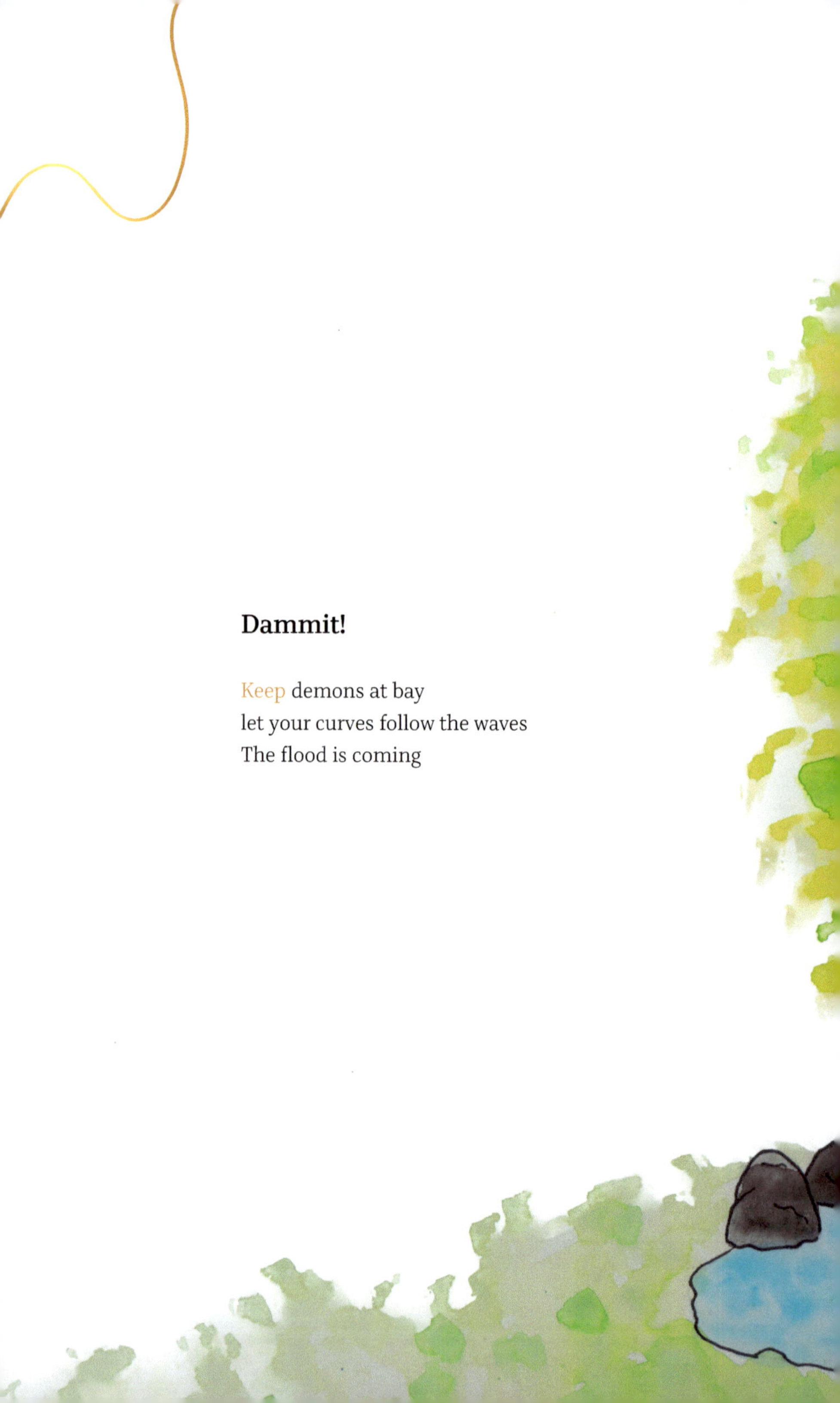

Dammit!

Keep demons at bay
let your curves follow the waves
The flood is coming

to Michael Joseph

There is still a poem I haven't written
And though I know that
I am just the vessel through which it comes
I have anchored myself in an ocean of ceaseless stillness
and motion
I stay in my seabed
unbothered by my qualified call
to walk along its surface

I've seen others attempt that walk
some drowned

in wav files
others' lifeboats were punctured

though
those who punctured their own lifeboats
were reborn
divinely filtered
among the salt of the earth

Alien blues' coup d'œil
(or Aunt Ester Tyler's Visit from the Black Autumn Ocean)

She asked why I don't share the sad stories

It's simple:

I enjoy making people smile.

If I share these writings
I lend the world my sorrows
It already knows so well

These words become immortalized
And, I am afraid
That even a Young 30 could add 30:
An Earthly decocture:
Green turns Blue

> *Ay! you are like a water to me, i can put you in my palm but cannot hold you
> nor the Wavy Blue Earth that bubbles up creating a tributary along our earthy
> cheeks*

> *Alas! A Tribune ascending away from tribunal responsibility*

> *We Decide.*
> *to carry these sorrows (with you)*
> *for the sorrows*
> *are not your own*
> *the Blue-Green is full of woke egos*

crowned.

Go to sleep, my child.

Ye is Us:

if you drown, We will catch your breath

We of the Black Autumn

are here

watching over you

So, what are you waiting for?

The world is not easy and there is no order of difficulty
Everything must be accepted, even the unacceptable

It simply is.

The Need to Want Four:
Edited Unabridged Black Autumnic Version

There is a confusion about the chase
That once the chase is done
ya know, nailed to the T
the *Chased* is simply no longer interested.

It is not so.
In fact, there is no chase at all, even.

Yes, it is a fact that it was not until she needed me to
want her did I not want her.

But there is a difference between fact and *truth*.

When she wanted me to want her
or in other words, when I wanted her (because we
were One, you see; Divinely attracted)
there was no need so *no-need* was attracted.

We chased our ethereal selves through the Being with.

There was no want, either.

Not really.
We were what we were in That moment and so we were
what we were in All moments.
It was One Felt-Knowledge.
We lived in a continuous now infinitely and eternally.

Death died. We were.

It wasn't until expressions were requested in fitting form that
they started disappearing.

It wasn't until I was asked to commit to
compromise
instead of committing to Love that
commitment needed effort.

That death returned as a reality reborn.

When Jerry hit the blue button on the
remote.

You know the feeling

A treasure chest turns into a
wastebin through perception alone.

You've been there

You know that feeling

When the chase ends.

When the connection is given a warrant
for Its arrest
for missing unscheduled court appearances
as if the chase were a trial and not already its
own capital punishment.

As if Love was not
   the only real Law and Lovelessness not
   the only real sin.

     And that that sin is not unlike
     swaddling yourselves
     in a cute blue fear-laced blanket
     that warms the body
     only by setting fire to its relationship
     with the mind.

     You know the feeling...

The need to want.

Perfect Love.

The Law is Perfect.

What have you given that has not been given to you?

They Sing

Their wings were flapping over my head
—Windless

No pull.

No push.

A Lightening before Dawn
Eye open and lips still

Seher Spoke

red, sacral, yellow, anahata, blue, ajna, and violet
spilled inside my wavelengths

And Now, We Are One.

And the Songs of the Black Gods were born

Cariño mioooo
Un beso tuyo una coronita de flores

BLACK
GITA

PURUSHA'S UNFOLDING

There is nothing but me. So what should i fear. I am
the rain. I am the tears.

Seher Speaks: The sons of the seas must change.

There's everything in me. So what should i crave.
I am the given. I am the gave. I am the living. I am
the grave. I am the cost. I am the paid.

Seher Speaks: The sons of the seas must change.

There is nothing but me. So why should i worry.
I am the rice. I am the curry. I am the full. I am the
hungry. I am the living. I am the Ghost. I am the
Still. I am the Host.

Seher Speaks: The sons of the seas must change.

There's everything in me. So why should i stress.
I am the worst. I am the best. I am the north. I am
the west. I am the Father. I am the Son. I am the sea.
I am the crumb.

Seher Speaks: The sons of the seas must change.

There's nothing but me. So why should i frown.
I am sky. I am ground. I am to. I am from. I am every
word. I am one. I am the Creator. I am the Created.
I am the incense meditating in fire. I am the
conditioned unconditional. I am awareness.
I am desire.

Seher Speaks: The sons of the seas must change.

There's everything in me. So why should i wait.
I am the wind and I am the water that gives birth to
the waves. I am the egg. I am the fate. I am the
One Moment impregnated with twins: Yesterday
and Today.

Seher Speaks: The sons of the seas must change.

There is nothing but me. So what could be taken.
I am filled. I am vacant. I am seed. I am soil. I am
the roots. I am the bloom. I am the space. I am the
room. I am the ink. I am the flow. I am the paper
and circling elbow.

Seher Speaks: The sons of the seas must change.

There's everything in me. So why should i struggle.
I am the phoenix. I am the rubble. I am that static.
I am the change. I am joy and the gift of pain. i am
woman. i am man. I am every grain of sand. I am the
Thought, Belief, and Action. I am the boat. I am the
captain.

Seher Speaks: The sons of the seas must change.

There is nothing but me. So why should I suffer.
I am the Fourth Truth. I am the Last Supper. I am
the pilgrimage. I am the Mecca. I am the Gītā. I am
Rosetta. I am *all about love* wrapped in *the power
of now* set aflame by *A Course in Miracles*. I am
Liberation in rhyme. I am the Changeless in
the Son of Moon's Shine.

Seher Speaks: The sons of the seas must change.

There is everything in Me. So of everything I am free.
I am God. I am Queen. My Father is Me.

Dawn Speaks: The sons of the seas is change.

There is no thing but me. So why should i fight.
There is no darkness.

I am Light

BLACK GITAS

Solstice

i write to immortalize my words
so that
when my shell breaks
my spirit continues speaking
reminding you
that
I am always here
and
I love you.

Yanna Marie Orcel

Yanna Marie Orcel is a multi-disciplinary visual artist, writer, performer, community organizer, and artist researcher. Throughout the Masters of Research program at Royal College of Art, she developed a curriculum, "Creative Care", which aims to bring together the Black community through collective creative expression sessions. The illustrator's credo asserts: "When you find yourself speechless or flooded with emotions, create art."

To stay up to date on this artist's creative work and research, follow her on Instagram at @Yannas_ArtStudio

www.ingramcontent.com/pod-product-compliance
Lightning Source LLC
Chambersburg PA
CBHW040944110726
48006CB00007B/1249